AERIAL VIEW OF PENNSYLVANIA
ISBN 1-55557-201-4 USED BY PERMISSION U.S. GEOLOGICAL SURVEY

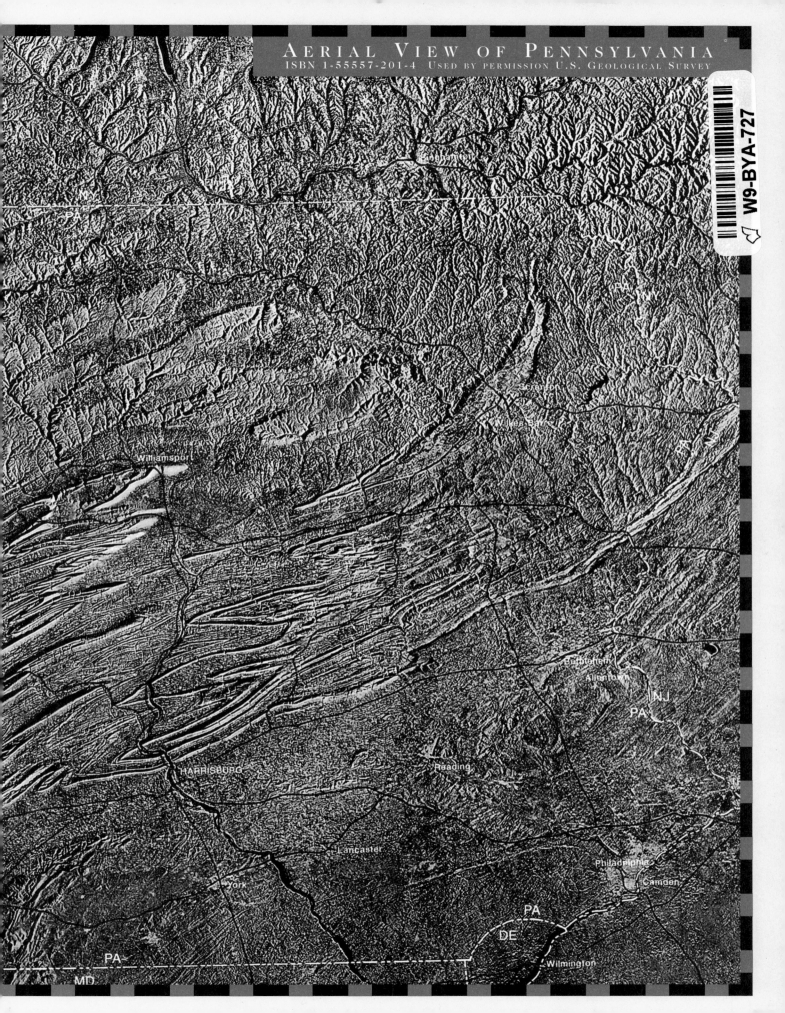

PENNSYLVANIA'S *tapestry*

SCENES FROM THE AIR

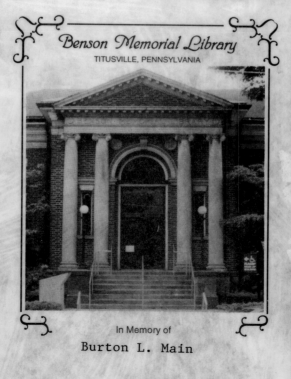

Benson Memorial Library
TITUSVILLE, PENNSYLVANIA

In Memory of
Burton L. Main

The Gift of
Tryonville Dutch Street Neighbors

Pennsylvania's Tapestry: Scenes from the Air
Text © 1999 by Ruth Hoover Seitz
Photography © 1999 by Blair Seitz
ISBN 1-879441-80-2
Library of Congress Catalog Card Number 98-067485

Published by

BOOKS

Seitz and Seitz, Inc.
1006 N. Second St.
Harrisburg, Pa 17102-3121
717-232-7944
FAX: 717-238-3280
www.celebratePA.com

Graphic Design by
Klinginsmith & Company

Printed in Hong Kong

PENNSYLVANIA'S
tapestry

SCENES FROM THE AIR

RB
BOOKS

"...richly beautiful"

Harrisburg, PA

RUTH HOOVER SEITZ • PHOTOGRAPHY BY BLAIR SEITZ

page 1: Morning fog hangs over the Juniata and Susquehanna River valleys, Perry County. *pages 2–3:* Raystown Lake, Huntingdon County, takes the shape of the river valley carved out by the Raystown branch of the Juniata River. *above:* Lake Wallenpaupack, Pike and Wayne Counties, is the largest of many lakes in the Poconos.

INTRODUCTION

Nature never stops. Its forces continuously alter the earth. Many acts that occur are minutia. For example, on the forest floor a lichen breaks down a rock, grain by grain.

Natural changes of a larger scale are seen by viewing the earth's topography from a plane. The lay of the land from the air opens a story that threads back 3.8 billion years to the planet's beginnings. Ever since, the earth's surface has been in action – erupting, thrusting, depositing, eroding, flowing, flooding, compressing, shifting, and tilting – many occurring in slow motion over millions of years.

Pennsylvania's geologic tale goes back 260 million years when Africa collided with North America. Among the following millenia is an epoch when the land that is now the Keystone State was situated over the equator and mostly under a warm sea. Very recently – only 26,000 years ago – a huge glacier moved south from Canada and affected much of the state. Human imagination can barely handle the lengths of time during which these enormous changes occurred. But we can enjoy the results – Pennsylvania's distinctive terrain.

Historical geologists have categorized Pennsylvania's surface features into seven physiographic provinces. Continuing the topographical pattern of eastern North America, the provinces angle from the southwest to the northeast. Together soil, rock, and water create a tapestry, beautiful in relief.

THE VARIED EAST 8
The ancient Delaware River carves through the Kittatinny Ridge past the Pocono Plateau to the west. Towards the southeast, rolling hills hold very old rock strata, mostly red in color, and the lowlands near Philadelphia mark an increase in human settlement.

THE RIDGE AND VALLEY MIDSTATE 30
The topography of the Ridge and Valley Province is cited in classrooms around the world as a classic example of geologic folding, now vividly displayed following long periods of erosion. The beauty of blue forested ridges interspersed by green agricultural valleys is a distinctive part of the state's tapestry.

THE APPALACHIAN PLATEAU WEST 78
The western part of Pennsylvania features hills of no particular pattern with both energetic and lazy rivers flowing between them. Many of the hills contain seams of coal formed approximately 300 million years before glaciation scoured parts of the Appalachian Plateau.

FROM THE PHOTOGRAPHER

Because of its varied topography, Pennsylvania is breathtaking to fly over at low altitudes. Its farms, forests, and waterways form lively patterns which change dramatically with the seasons. On a clear day from 3,000 feet above in a Cessna 172, mountains, rivers, roads, and plowed fields fill the picture frame in expansive panoramas. Lower, at 1,000 feet, one or two of the features become dominant, on a canvas of strong shapes, textures, and color.

I have not attempted to photograph every feature of the state. In particular, I have skipped over the sprawling suburbs we have built around our towns and cities. I do not find the black asphalt of our large shopping mall parking lots and football field wide roofs of our single-level, corporate centers pleasing to photograph.

Instead, I have focused my lens for this book on what we have to preserve with pride—our wild lands, farms, and open countryside as well as our historic towns and cities. I celebrate that Pennsylvania's forests and open lands in some areas stretch as far as the eye can see.

In a 250-mile sweep from Bedford County in the southwest to Lackawanna County in the northeast, Pennsylvania exhibits the world's best examples of ridge and valley topography. I have devoted extra photographs to this central area of the state.

–Blair Seitz

left: At sunset, the photographer completes a photo flight aboard a Cessna 172 rented with a skilled pilot from the Harrisburg Jet Center. *above:* Farms occupy the valleys between midstate mountain ridges, Bedford County.

THE VARIED EAST

Although commonly called the Pocono Mountains, much of the the Poconos is a plateau composed of hard sandstone rock in the Appalachian Plateaus Province. From the air, the land from Jim Thorpe in Carbon County east to Camelback Mountain and north to Lake Wallenpaupack looks like a tableland. Glaciation and erosion by water created this flat, elevated area dotted with lakes and bogs.

Farther south in Northampton County, the form of the topography is part of the classic Ridge and Valley Province that makes up most of the midstate. Flat and limestone-rich, the Great Valley encompasses valuable agricultural land. South of the Lehigh Valley, a portion of the Great Valley, rises a narrow segment of the Reading Prong, a landscape with rounded hills carved out of very ancient rocks. Berks County's Mount Penn is an example.

The Piedmont Province stretches from Northwest Philadelphia north to upper Bucks County and then west to Adams. Here some of the oldest rocks in the state are closest to the surface. From the heart of Chester, Montgomery, and Bucks Counties have come building stones such as granite, slate, and serpentine that were metamorphosed by extreme heat and pressure more than 570 million years ago. At that time, sedimentation and volcanic thrust impacted a Pennsylvania land mass that—unbelievably—was tilted towards the southeast and situated over the equator.

In this province are also younger 200-million-year-old rocks such as red, sedimentary rocks that show up in low, undulating portions of northern Bucks, western Lancaster, and southern Adams Counties and hard, gray diabase rocks that form low hills in the same area.

The Delaware River flows through terrain where rocks vary in age by more than 500 million years. When it first enters Pennsylvania, the upper Delaware flows over bedrock, creating rapids. Beyond this scenic ruggedness, the river slows to a gentle flow until it dramatically cuts through the Kittatinny Ridge, the tailbone of the Appalachians. Geologists surmise that the river carved through a weakness, possibly a fault, in this ridge that runs north into New Jersey and south into Virginia. On the heels of erosion extended over millions of years, the stunning Delaware Water Gap was created.

On its southward journey to the Atlantic, the river becomes navigable near its mouth. From the air, it is obvious that flatlands, accessible by their nature, became magnets for settlements. Philadelphia swells the lowlands where the Schuylkill River joins the Delaware and flows towards the Atlantic. Most of the city rests on sandy, level terrain of the Atlantic Coastal Plain Province.

From the Pocono plateau to the Philadelphia lowlands, the physiography of eastern Pennsylvania demonstrates maturity and variety.

page 8: Interstate 80 uses the natural opening formed by the Delaware River at the Delaware Water Gap, Monroe County. *above:* Two covered bridges cross Buck and Doe Runs in the Laurels Reserve, Chester County. *right:* Fall leaves and sunset enhance the Delaware River's beauty at Dingmans Ferry, Pike County.

previous pages: Philadelphia, Pennsylvania's largest city, is situated along the lower Delaware River. *above:* The Schuylkill River cuts through West Philadelphia where the Philadelphia Museum of Art is located (center) at the end of the Benjamin Franklin Parkway. *right:* The town of Womelsdorf is a commerce center for surrounding farms, Berks County.

previous pages: Contour farming makes tapestry-like patterns, Lehigh County. *above, right and next page:* The mixed cropping as well as contour farming in Pennsylvania's valleys provides artistic designs, Berks County.

above: Lake Nockamixon, Bucks County, draws sailboat enthusiasts to Nockamixon State Park. *left:* Easton, the easternmost city of the Lehigh Valley metropolitan area, is bordered on the south by the Lehigh River and on the east by the Delaware.

above: Horse and cattle farms grace the rolling countryside of Chester County where efforts of conservancy groups are preserving open space.

above: The deep colors of the
fall foliage border Lake Paupack
in Promised Land State Park,
Pike County.

previous page: Farms surround recreational Blue Marsh Lake, Berks County. *above:* Resort centers abound in the lake-rich vacation area of the Pocono Plateau. *right:* Just south of Milford, the Delaware River is the boundary between Pennsylvania (left) and New Jersey (right).

THE RIDGE AND VALLEY MIDSTATE

One of central Pennsylvania's characteristic scenic features is its soft blue ridges and the intervening valleys marked by towns and farms. On a clear day it is rewarding to hike to an overlook and view the mountains and valleys that lie nearly parallel. For instance, from Blue Mountain in Dauphin County, successive ridges – Second, Stony, and Peter's Mountains – line up towards the northeast in receding tones of blue with valleys of varying widths between. An aerial view strikingly exposes fingers of woodland protruding down from the dark, tree-filled ridges and extending into the carefully contoured fields of the valleys. When the valleys narrow, there is less cultivation.

The forms of the ridges vary, some converging, others diverging. Rock outcroppings occasionally crest a ridge. Some ridges loop; others widen with frilly crinkles caused by erosion. All of the tree-covered ridges appear cuddly soft from an overhead view. Lookout ridges such as Hawk Mountain of the Kittatinny offer a boon for migrating raptors. The birds glide on updrafts created by winds striking the ridges.

This pattern is repeated across a broad swath reaching northeastward into New Jersey and southwestward into Maryland. This tapestry of alternating ridges and valleys is aligned with the

Appalachian Mountain chain that runs 1,600 miles from Alabama to Quebec.

Cataclysmic activity produced the Ridge and Valley Province as we know it today. Erosion of mountains long since gone produced sand and mud that was deposited in an ancient Appalachian sea. These materials were cemented into rocks that were jolted during the collision of Africa and North America 260 million years ago. As a result, the rocks were folded just as a flexible throw rug bends when it is pushed at one end. The earth's crust was bent down and up, and the layers of rock were crumpled by pressure. The folding was a single continuous event that occurred over a period of 20 to 40 million years.

Since the folding, erosion gradually wore down the folds of uplifted rock. The ridges today are sides, or limbs, of anticlines and synclines, those sinuous creases that plunge to a deeper level than is visible from the air. In many instances, only one side of a fold is obvious.

According to Dr. William D. Sevon, geologist at the Bureau of Topographic and Geologic Survey in the Pennsylvania Department of Conservation and Natural Resources, the midstate topography is a prime example of the ridge and valley physiography. Extensive erosion has clearly defined the ridges and the valleys. The steep wooded slopes of the ridges are upheld by resistant sandstones, with quartzite, a tough mineral, the rocks' main ingredient. The adjacent valleys were created when softer rock such as shales and limestones were worn away.

It is in the valleys that farms abound. Northampton County, southern Dauphin County, and Lebanon County are all part of the Great Valley, an expansive area that reaches from Easton past

Chambersburg, south to the Maryland border. Its populated areas such as Allentown, Hershey, Harrisburg, and Shippensburg are all built on flat stretches with the rich soil of the outlying terrain excellent for farming.

Appealing field patterns result from the conservation savvy of twentieth century farmers. From the air, it appears that colorful strips and contours rotate at the artistic whimsy of the farmer. In reality, agronomists from the Natural Resources Conservation Service recommend each pattern based on the form of the land. Alternating row and broadcast crops, this method of cultivation prevents soil erosion, saves fuel, and conserves water. As the seasons progress, April greens become a tapestry of July yellows. Freshly plowed swaths, less common as farmers adopt minimum-till practices to reduce soil exposure, add earth tones to the design.

Like the Delaware in the east, the Susquehanna River surprisingly cuts through ridges and valleys as it flows toward the Chesapeake Bay. Old and venerable, the origins of this river are obscured by the mists of time. Now its bends give a scenic view to hikers, canoeists, and pilots. Its morning fog wards off frost, lengthening the growing season on riverine farms. Unfortunately, it also periodically floods its shoreline communities with devastating force. Dotting the landscape, dams, lakes, and reservoirs play a role in flood prevention.

Few dramatic, large-scale, earth-changing events are happening now in Pennsylvania, explains Dr. Sevon. "The main active geological force now at work in the state is isostatic uplift. When soil material is eroded from the surface of the Commonwealth and carried away by one of its many rivers, there is a gradual uplift of that surface to compensate for the loss." Erosion has given the folds produced by the ancient upheaval new forms in an area that is today strikingly beautiful and very Pennsylvanian.

pages 30–31: Railroad, highway, and walking bridges traverse the Susquehanna River at Harrisburg. *page 32:* Mifflin County's "Big Valley" as locally known is wide and flat near Belleville. *page 33:* The town of Mount Union, Huntingdon County, is located in the midstate's ridge and valley region. *above:* This high view of Harrisburg shows the residential area from State Street south to Paxton Street and the city center. *right:* Pennsylvania's capitol sits on a hill up from the Susquehanna River and boasts recent fountain, gardens, and east wing additions.

above: North of Harrisburg, the intersections of Route 322, Interstate 81 and several access streets form a concrete web. *right:* The Harrisburg Senators play AA baseball on City Island as boats ply the Susquehanna River along Harrisburg's midtown.

previous pages: The Juniata River (left) and Route 322 (right) run east then turn north in Perry County northwest of Harrisburg. Summer haze softens the ridges and valleys. *above and top right:* Farms of northern Dauphin County lie in the flatlands between mountain ridges east of Millersburg and the Susquehanna River. *bottom right:* Route 283 highway traverses western Lancaster County farmland.

above and right: Fields in Pennsylvania make many different designs depending on the farm's topography. A farm in Northumberland County (above) utilizes the contours of the hill the farm is built on, while the farms in Lebanon County (top right) and in Mifflin County (right) create other designs. Corn and grain crops are interspersed in planting.

previous page: The flat, fertile farmland of Lebanon County is part of Pennsylvania's section of the "great valley" which extends from the south into parts of Franklin, Cumberland, Dauphin, Berks, Lehigh, and Northampton Counties. above: Gifford Pinchot State Park, York County, like many parks across the state, includes a lake formed from damming a creek. right above: Ridges and valleys are the topography characteristic of the midstate, seen here in the fall, Cumberland County (foreground). right and next pages: Frost and fog hang in the valleys of Perry County south of Newport.

left: Early morning fog lifts from farms in the midstate. *above:* Route 322 passes Laurel Creek Dam in Mifflin Country. Ridges of Centre County rise in the background at sunset.

previous pages: Sunset reflects on the Susquehanna River's West Branch in Clinton County looking northwest from Hyner. *above:* The Juniata River (bottom) joins the Susquehanna River at the bridges at Clarks Ferry (left) and Duncannon (right). *right:* Interstate 81 Bridge spans the Susquehanna north of Harrisburg.

previous pages 56–57: Dickinson College campus exhibits its fall beauty in the town of Carlisle, Cumberland County. *left:* Scenic Route 6 stretches across northern Pennsylvania, here at Wyalusing Rocks overlooking the Susquehanna River, Bradford County. *right:* Churches stand out in the northern sector of Towanda bordered by the Susquehanna River, Bradford County.

previous pages: Several villages are situated along Pine Creek in Lycoming County. *above:* Pine Creek Gorge, known also as the Grand Canyon of Pennsylvania, cuts dramatically into the mountains of Tioga County.

above: The gorge holding Pine Creek appears at the top of this fall foliage scene near Leonard Harrison State Park on the canyon's eastern rim, Tioga County.

previous pages 62–63: Located southwest of Altoona, the Horseshoe Curve on the Philadelphia to Pittsburgh rail line follows the shape of the mountain. *left:* In Lancaster County an Amish funeral procession approaches the cemetery. *above:* Amish farms can be identified because they do not have electrical power lines, Lancaster County.

above: The town of Pittston is situated along the Susquehanna River between Wilkes–Barre and Scranton. *right:* Built when rail transport was dominant, the Tunkhannock Viaduct spans a valley in northeast Wyoming County.

above: The Susquehanna River forms the boundary between Wrightsville, York (left) and Columbia, Lancaster (right) Counties. *right*: Orchards and springtime apple blossoms abound in Adams County.

previous pages: On a summer evening, motorboats speed along the irregular shores of Raystown Lake, Huntingdon County. *above:* The West and North branches of the Susquehanna River join at Sunbury (right) and Northumberland (top center). *right:* Over Altoona, looking north along 17th Street, the Blair County Courthouse (at top of picture) marks the town center. *pages 76–77:* Blanketed in fresh snow, a Bedford County farm stands in the U-turn of the Juniata River, Raystown Branch.

THE APPALACHIAN PLATEAU WEST

Aged hills, winding rivers, and connecting lakes and creeks are landmarks of western Pennsylvania. Except for a narrow band of land along Lake Erie, this region is within the largest physiographic region in Pennsylvania, the Appalachian Plateaus Province. It extends from Greene and Fayette Counties along the West Virginia border north to Erie and to Wayne and Pike Counties in the northeast.

From the air, much of the area appears mountainous because of deep erosion by streams and rivers that follow the slope of the land. For example, from the Seneca Point fire tower in Cook Forest State Park, one can look down on the Clarion River looping gracefully among the hills within its watershed. Farther south, the Allegheny River makes a majestic curve at East Brady in Armstrong County. For part of this sweeping bend, the riverbed meanders at the base of five-hundred-foot bluffs.

The bedrock of the Appalachian Plateaus Province characteristically remains relatively flat with broad folds and few faults because the rock strata were not affected as severely by the mountain-building that created the folds of the Ridge and Valley. These rocks are formed from sediments deposited more than 300 million years ago. Pressure from the weight of rock compressed wood debris, known as peat, to produce seams of coal. Other more obscure processes produced oil and natural gas.

The Appalachian Plateaus Province has abundant woods growing on younger rock formations. Its forests include the Laurel Highlands, Pine Creek Gorge, and the 500,000-acre Allegheny National Forest. From the air, the mountains of the west seem less defined than the sandstone ridges of the Ridge and Valley Province to the east.

The state's highest point, Mt. Davis, 3,213 feet, is part of Negro Mountain situated in the Appalachian Plateaus Province. This peak occurs on the crest of an anticline that has yet to be eroded to form ridges. Within the same county, the Pennsylvania Turnpike cuts through Negro Mountain, revealing coal in the bedrock in its core.

The northwestern part of the Appalachian Plateaus Province has been greatly affected by glaciation. The most recent ice sheet entered Pennsylvania from the north about 24,000 years ago. This continental glacier reversed the direction of rivers so that instead of flowing northward into the St. Lawrence, they wind southwest into the Ohio River.

The ice flows also broke up large amounts of rock. Some of this rock now occurs as boulders strewn in Slippery Rock Creek Gorge and some of it was pulverized into the glacial sand on Lake Erie's peninsula, Presque Isle. As the ice receded, its melting formed Lake Erie and some other smaller lakes that add to Pennsylvania's scenic topography.

page 79: The Clarion River makes one of its horseshoe turns in Cook Forest State Park, at the intersection of Clarion, Forest and Jefferson Counties. *above:* In this picture above Jefferson County, cleared farmland is bounded by forest.

above: Recreational lakes were
built at most of Pennsylvania's 114
state parks, Prince Gallitzin State
Park, Cambria County.

above and right: Due to higher elevation, winter snows are more frequent at these farms in Somerset County.

above: Athletic fields of this Somerset County town provide a community meeting place. *right:* In the state's western highland region, forest and farms are interspersed, Clearfield County.

previous pages 86 and 87: The Youghiogheny River has cut a deep valley in the highlands of southwest Pennsylvania, Somerset County. *left top:* Presque Isle State Park is a thin arm of land, abundant with wildlife, jutting into Lake Erie at the town of Erie. *left:* Shared with Ohio, Pymatuning Reservoir has a shore line of some 40 miles and provides varied habitat for many bird species. The Pennsylvania sector is Pymatuning State Park, Crawford County. *above:* In the northwest, Allegheny Reservoir, located in Warren and McKean Counties in the Allegheny National Forest, extends into New York state.

previous pages: The Allegheny (left) and the Monongahela (right) Rivers join to form the Ohio River at Pittsburgh's Point Park. *above:* Above the Allegheny River this view looks southeast toward Ford City, Armstrong County. *right:* Locks for barges and a steel-truss bridge span the Monongahela River at North Charleroi, Washington County.

above: From 2,000 feet above, homes on the hills across the Monongahela River contrast with the skyscrapers of downtown Pittsburgh. *right:* This steel mill along the Monongahela River at Clairton south of Pittsburgh continues manufacturing. *page 96:* Well–kept productive farms dominate the countryside, Somerset County.